GW01086892

HAIDA

OUT OF THE SILENCE

KWAKIUTL

OUT OF THE SILENCE

PHOTOGRAPHS BY ADELAIDE DE MENIL
TEXT BY WILLIAM REID

PUBLISHED FOR THE AMON CARTER MUSEUM, FORT WORTH
BY HARPER & ROW, PUBLISHERS
NEW YORK, EVANSTON, SAN FRANCISCO, LONDON

THE AMON CARTER MUSEUM WAS ESTABLISHED IN 1961 UNDER THE WILL OF THE LATE AMON G. CARTER FOR THE STUDY AND DOCUMENTATION OF WESTERING NORTH AMERICA. THE PROGRAM OF THE MUSEUM, EXPRESSED IN PUBLICATIONS, EXHIBITIONS, AND PERMANENT COLLECTIONS, REFLECTS MANY ASPECTS OF AMERICAN CULTURE, BOTH HISTORIC AND CONTEMPORARY.

WHEN WE LOOK AT A PARTICULAR WORK
OF NORTHWEST COAST ART
AND SEE THE SHAPE OF IT,
WE ARE ONLY LOOKING AT ITS AFTER-LIFE.
ITS REAL LIFE IS THE MOVEMENT
BY WHICH IT GOT TO BE THAT SHAPE.

TSIMSHIAN

IT'S EASY TO BECOME ENTRANCED
BY THE SOFT CURTAIN OF AGE,
SEEING THIS
INSTEAD OF WHAT IT OBSCURES.

HAIDA

AN UGLY BUILDING
CAN MAKE A BEAUTIFUL RUIN,
AND A BEAUTIFUL MASK
IN THE DARK OF MANY YEARS,
SOFTENED BY WEAR,
BECOMES A SYMBOL WHICH TELLS US
THAT THE CYCLE OF LIFE,
DEATH, DECAY AND RE-BIRTH
IS A NATURAL AND BEAUTIFUL ONE.

HAIDA

HAIDA

THIS IS NOT WHAT THEIR CREATORS INTENDED.

HAIDA

THESE WERE OBJECTS OF BRIGHT PRIDE,
TO BE ADMIRED
IN THE NEWNESS
OF THEIR CRISP CURVED LINES,
THE POWERFUL FLOW
OF SURE ELEGANT CURVES AND RECESSES
-YES, AND IN THE BRIGHTNESS
OF FRESH PAINT.

THEY TOLD THE PEOPLE
OF THE COMPLETENESS OF THEIR CULTURE,
THE CONTINUING LINEAGES OF THE GREAT FAMILIES
THEIR CLOSENESS TO THE MAGIC WORLD
OF MYTH AND LEGEND.

TSIMSHIAN

KWAKIUTL

PERHAPS THEY TOLD MORE,
A STORY OF LITTLE PEOPLE,
FEW IN SCATTERED NUMBERS,
IN A HUGE DARK WORLD
OF ENORMOUS FORESTS
OF ABSURDLY LARGE TREES,
AND STORMY COASTS
AND WILD WATERS BEYOND,
WHERE BRIEF COOL SUMMERS
GAVE WAY FOREVER
TO LONG BLACK WINTERS,
AND FAMILIES ROUND THEIR FIRES,
NO MATTER HOW LONG THEIR LINEAGES,
NEEDED MUCH ASSURANCE
OF THEIR GREATNESS.

HAIDA

THE WONDER OF IT ALL
IS THAT THERE WERE SO FEW—
A HANDFUL OF SEA-HUNTERS
CLINGING TO TINY FOOTHOLDS
ON THE JUNGLE-BACKED BEACHES.

BUT
IT WAS A RICH LAND,

HAIDA

TLINGIT

ABOVE ALL,
A RICH SEA.

MILLIONS OF SALMON RETURNED EACH YEAR
TO THE RIVERS
TO SPAWN AND DIE,
A SACRIFICE
THAT ASSURED THE SURVIVAL OF THEIR KIND,
AND AT THE SAME TIME
GAVE EASY LIFE
TO THE BEAR, THE OTTER, THE EAGLE,
AND A HOST OF OTHERS,
A FEW OF WHOM WERE HUMANS.

IN A FEW WEEKS,
MEN COULD GATHER
ENOUGH SALMON
TO LAST A YEAR.
SHELLFISH
GREW THICK ON THE ROCKS
AND SANDY BOTTOMS;
HALIBUT
CARPETED THE SHELF FLOOR;
BERRIES
WERE PLENTIFUL
ON THE BARE HILLSIDES;
AND IF
THERE WEREN'T ENOUGH
BARE HILLSIDES,
A FIRE
ON A HOT DAY
WOULD PROVIDE ONE
FOR THE NEXT YEAR.

KWAKIUTL

KWAKIUTL

SEA LION AND SEA OTTER,
SEAL AND WHALE AND PORPOISE
WERE EVERYWHERE,
AND ALL FLESH WAS MEAT.

IN THE EARLY SPRING
THE RIVERS SWARMED WITH OOLICHAN,
THE MAGIC FISH OF THE NORTH COAST,
NINETY PERCENT OIL
AND, TO THOSE WHO KNEW IT WELL,
FRAGRANT, DELICIOUS OIL
TO ENHANCE THE FLAVOR
OF DRIED SALMON AND HALIBUT,
TO MIX WITH DRIED BERRIES,
TO FLAVOR STEWS,
AND, THOUGH THEY DID NOT KNOW THIS,
TO PROVIDE MOST OF THE STORED NUTRIENTS
NECESSARY FOR LIFE
IN THE TOO-OFTEN SUNLESS SEASONS.

TLINGIT

THERE WERE NETTLE ROOTS
AND WATER LILY ROOTS
AND SEAWEEDS,
GULL EGGS,
BLACK BEAR,
GRIZZLY BEAR,
DEER,
AND MUCH MORE,
RIGHT THERE FOR THE TAKING.

TLINGIT

IF THE SEA HUNT WERE UNSUCCESSFUL
OR SMOKED FISH RAN OUT
BEFORE THE NEW SEASON ARRIVED,
MUSSELS WERE A DARK BLUE MANTLE
ON ALMOST ANY ROCK,
COCKLES LAY EXPOSED AT LOW TIDE,
ABALONE AND ROCK OYSTERS
COULD BE FOUND WITH LITTLE EFFORT,
TIDE POOLS YIELDED DELICATE SEA URCHINS,
THE OCTOPUS COULD BE FLUSHED FROM HIS CAVE,
AND CLAMS LAY UNDER MOST BEACHES.

TLINGIT

EVEN TODAY,
ONLY A STUPID MAN
COULD STARVE ON THIS COAST,
AND TODAY
IS NOT AS IT WAS.

HAIDA

THEN
THERE WAS THE FOREST.

NOWHERE ELSE
WAS THERE ANYTHING
LIKE THE DOUGLAS FIR,
THE STRONGEST, TOUGHEST,
IN MANY WAYS MOST REMARKABLE
WOOD IN THE WORLD.

HAIDA

TREES SIX, EIGHT,
TWELVE FEET THROUGH THE BUTT,
FORTY OR FIFTY FEET TO THE FIRST LIMBS,
TWO OR THREE HUNDRED FEET TALL.

THEY ARE NEARLY ALL GONE NOW,
BUT FOR AWHILE
THEY PROVIDED
THE BEAMS AND UPRIGHTS AND SIDING
FOR HALF THE HOUSES OF AMERICA,
AND SUPPORTS FOR MANY BIG BUILDINGS.

HAIC

BUT TO BE USED,
THEY HAD TO WAIT FOR THE WHITE MAN
AND HIS STEEL AXES AND SAWS.
THEY WERE JUST TOO TOUGH
AND HARD AND HEAVY
FOR THE STONE AXE
AND WOODEN WEDGE.

TSIMSHIAN

THE SPRUCE AND HEMLOCK
WERE SPLINTERY AND HARD TO WORK
AND WEATHERED BADLY.
SO A RICHNESS IN TIMBER
LAY UNTOUCHED AND USELESS
TILL THE WHITE MAN CAME.
IF THIS HAD BEEN ALL,
THESE PEOPLE
MIGHT HAVE DEGENERATED
TO SIMPLE DEPENDENCE
ON FOOD RESOURCES.

BUT THERE WAS THE CEDAR,
THE WEST COAST CYPRESS,
GROWING HUGE AND PLENTIFUL
IN SWAMPY AREAS
AROUND CREEKS AND RIVERS.

TLINGIT

OH, THE CEDAR TREE!

IF MANKIND IN HIS INFANCY
HAD PRAYED FOR THE PERFECT SUBSTANCE
FOR ALL MATERIAL AND AESTHETIC NEEDS,
AN INDULGENT GOD COULD HAVE PROVIDED
NOTHING BETTER. BEAUTIFUL IN ITSELF,
WITH A MAGNIFICENT FLARED BASE
TAPERING SUDDENLY TO A TALL, STRAIGHT TRUNK
WRAPPED IN REDDISH BROWN BARK,
LIKE A GREAT COAT OF GENTLE FUR,
GRACEFULLY SWEEPING BOUGHS,
SOFT FEATHERY FRONDS OF GRAY GREEN NEEDLES.

HUGE, SOME OF THESE CEDARS,
FIVE HUNDRED YEARS OF SLOW GROWTH,
TOWERING FROM THEIR MASSIVE BASES.

HAIDA

HAIDA

THE WOOD IS SOFT,
BUT OF A WONDERFUL FIRMNESS
AND, IN A GOOD TREE,
SO STRAIGHT-GRAINED
IT WILL SPLIT TRUE AND CLEAN
INTO FORTY FOOT PLANKS,
FOUR INCHES THICK
AND THREE FEET WIDE,
WITH SCARCELY A KNOT.

ACROSS THE GRAIN
IT CUTS CLEAN AND PRECISE.
IT IS LIGHT IN WEIGHT
AND BEAUTIFUL IN COLOR,
REDDISH BROWN WHEN NEW,
SILVERY GREY WHEN OLD.

IT IS PERMEATED WITH NATURAL OILS
THAT MAKE IT ONE OF THE LONGEST LASTING
OF ALL WOODS,
EVEN IN THE DAMP
OF THE NORTHWEST COAST CLIMATE.

TLINGIT

WHEN STEAMED
IT WILL BEND WITHOUT BREAKING.
IT WILL MAKE HOUSES AND BOATS
AND BOXES AND COOKING POTS.
ITS BARK WILL MAKE MATS,
EVEN CLOTHING.
WITH A FEW BITS
OF SHARPENED STONE AND ANTLER,
WITH SOME BEAVER TEETH
AND A LOT OF TIME,
WITH LATER ON A BIT OF IRON,
YOU CAN BUILD FROM THE CEDAR TREE
THE EXTERIOR TRAPPINGS
OF ONE OF THE WORLD'S GREAT CULTURES.

ABOVE ALL,
YOU CAN BUILD TOTEM POLES,
AND THE PEOPLE OF THE NORTHWEST COAST
BUILT THEM IN PROFUSION:
FORESTS OF SCULPTURED COLUMNS
BETWEEN THEIR HOUSES AND THE SEA,
PROUDLY ANNOUNCING TO ALL
THE HERALDIC PAST OF THOSE WHO DWELT THERE.

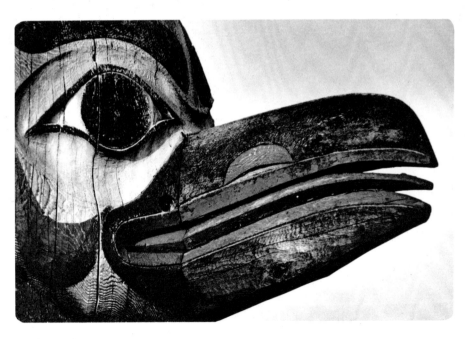

TLINGIT

AT MOST, THERE WERE PROBABLY NO MORE
THAN A HUNDRED THOUSAND PEOPLE,
SCATTERED ALONG
A THOUSAND MILES OF COASTLINE
-TEN THOUSAND MILES MORE LIKELY-
IF BAYS AND INLETS
AND PROMONTORIES AND ISLANDS
WERE MEASURED.
ISOLATED IN CLUSTERS OF A FEW HUNDRED EACH,
MILES FROM THEIR NEAREST NEIGHBORS,
CUT OFF BY DENSE JUNGLES,
BY STORMY SEAS FOR MOST OF THE YEAR,
BY FIVE SEPARATE LANGUAGE GROUPS
AND HUNDREDS OF DISTINCT DIALECTS,
AND BY SUSPICIONS AND ANIMOSITIES
THAT OFTEN SEPARATED THEM
MORE THAN THE ELEMENTS.

WHAT CAN A FEW PEOPLE DO,
EXCEPT CLING TO A MARGINAL EXISTENCE?

HAIDA

AND YET

-ONE OF THESE CLUSTERS WAS TANU.
IT WASN'T EVEN A SINGLE POLITICAL ENTITY,
BUT TWO VILLAGES
SEPARATED BY ONLY A FEW YARDS.

HAIDA

IT KNEW NO LAW
BEYOND CUSTOM,
NO HISTORY
BEYOND LEGEND,
NO POLITICAL UNIT
LARGER THAN THE FAMILY,
NO GOVERNMENT
BEYOND AN INFORMAL MEETING OF FAMILY HEADS,
PLUS THE TACIT ACCEPTANCE
OF THE SUPERIORITY OF THE RANKING CHIEF.

HAIDA

HAIDA

AT THE HEIGHT OF ITS INFLUENCE,
IT HAD LESS THAN A THOUSAND PEOPLE
LIVING IN ABOUT TWENTY-FIVE HOUSES.

BUT IF THE WOODEN STRUCTURES OF TANU
HAD SURVIVED THE HUNDRED YEARS
OF NORTH COAST WEATHER
SINCE THE LAST OF ITS SURVIVORS LEFT,
ITS RUINS WOULD RIVAL
MAN'S GREATEST ACHIEVEMENTS.
TANU MAY HAVE BEEN THE CROWNING GEM
OF WEST COAST MATERIAL CULTURE.
SOME OLD MEMORIES STILL RECALL
ITS ARTISTS AND BUILDERS AS THE BEST,
AND OLD PHOTOGRAPHS
SHOW SOMETHING OF ITS GLORY.
BUT IT WAS ONLY ONE
OF DOZENS OF PROUD CITADELS-
KAISUN, KIUSTA, SQUONQUAI, SKIDEGATE,
MASSETT, KITWANCOOL, KISPIOX, GITSIXUKLA,
KITWANGA, KINCOLITH, KASAAN, KLUKWAN,
BELLA BELLA, BELLA COOLA,
KOSKIMO, QUATSINO, NOOTKA,
AND MANY MORE.

HAIDA

IN EACH VILLAGE WERE GREAT HOUSES
SOME SEVENTY FEET BY FIFTY FEET
OF CLEAR ROOF SPAN,
WITH GRACEFULLY FLUTED POSTS AND BEAMS.
IN THE HOUSES THERE WAS WEALTH
-NOT GOLD OR PRECIOUS STONES-
BUT TREASURES THAT ONLY GREAT TRADITIONS,
TALENT, AND SOMETIMES GENIUS,
WITH UNLIMITED TIME AND DEVOTION,
CAN CREATE.

HAIDA

TSIMSHIAN

THERE WERE TREASURES IN PROFUSION
-THOUSANDS OF MASKS,
PAINTED AND CARVED CHESTS,
RATTLES, DISHES,
UTENSILS OF ALL KINDS,
CEREMONIAL REGALIA-
ALL CAREFULLY STORED
OR PROUDLY DISPLAYED
DURING THE GREAT FEASTS
AND WINTER CEREMONIES.

TSIMSHIAN

THE PEOPLE OF
THE NORTHWEST COAST
WERE RICH.

THEIR SEA EVEN RICHER;
THEY WERE ENORMOUSLY ENERGETIC,
AND THEY CENTERED THEIR SOCIETY
AROUND WHAT WAS TO THEM
THE ESSENCE OF LIFE:
WHAT WE NOW CALL "ART".

TSIMSHIAN

HAIDA

OLD PEOPLE CAN STILL TELL "HOW IT WAS"
WHEN, BY BOAT, THEY ROUNDED A POINT OF LAND
AND ENTERED A SHELTERED BAY
TO FIND A VILLAGE OF LARGE HOUSES
AND TOTEM POLES FACING THE SEA.

HAIDA

LIKE HERALDIC CRESTS,
THESE POLES TOLD
OF THE MYTHOLOGICAL BEGINNINGS
OF THE GREAT FAMILIES,
AT A TIME BEFORE TIME,
WHEN ANIMALS AND MYTHIC BEASTS AND MEN
LIVED AS EQUALS,
AND ALL THAT WAS TO BE
WAS ESTABLISHED BY THE PLAY
OF RAVEN AND EAGLE,
BEAR AND WOLF,
FROG AND BEAVER,
THUNDERBIRD AND WHALE.

KWAKIUTL

TSIMSHIAN

THE POLES WERE MANY THINGS.
THE HOUSE POLE
TOLD OF THE LINEAGE OF THE CHIEF
WHO PRESIDED WITHIN.
THE MEMORIAL POLE
COMMEMORATED SOME GREAT EVENT.
THE GRAVE POLE
CONTAINED THE BODY
AND DISPLAYED THE CREST
OF A LEADING NOBLE.

IN MANY OF THE GREAT HOUSES,
MASSIVE FIGURES
-ILLUMINATED BY FIRELIGHT-
SUPPORTED THE ROOF BEAMS.

TLINGIT

TLINGIT

TLINGIT

EACH POLE CONTAINED THE ESSENTIAL SPIRIT
OF THE INDIVIDUAL OR FAMILY
IT COMMEMORATED,
AS WELL AS THE SPIRIT
OF THE ARTIST WHO MADE IT,
AND, BY AN EXTENSION,
THE LIVING ESSENCE OF THE WHOLE PEOPLE.
WHILE THE PEOPLE LIVED,
THE POLES LIVED,
AND LONG AFTER THEIR CULTURE DIED,
THE POLES CONTINUED TO RADIATE
A TERRIBLE VITALITY
THAT ONLY DECAY AND DESTRUCTION COULD END.

EVEN TRAPPED
IN THE STAIRWELLS OF MUSEUMS,
TRUNCATED AND DISMEMBERED
IN STORAGE SHEDS,
OR LYING IN SHATTERED FRAGMENTS
IN NOW VANISHED VILLAGES
THEY ONCE GLORIFIED,
THE CONTAINED POWER
-BORN OF MAGIC ORIGINS
AND THE GENIUS OF THEIR CREATORS -
STILL SURVIVES.
ALL THINGS MUST DIE,
AND GREAT ART MUST BE A LIVING THING,
OR IT IS NOT ART AT ALL.

HAIDA

HAIDA

THESE MONUMENTS WERE THE WORK
OF MASTER CARVERS AND APPRENTICES
WHO BROUGHT TO FINAL PERFECTION
AN ART STYLE WHOSE ORIGINS
LAY DEEP IN THE PAST AND PARTLY IN ASIA.

IT WAS AN AUSTERE, SOPHISTICATED ART.
ITS PREVAILING MOOD WAS CLASSICAL CONTROL,
YET IT CHARACTERIZED
EVEN THE SIMPLEST OBJECTS OF DAILY LIFE.
THESE SEA - GOING HUNTERS
TOOK THE ENTIRE ENVIRONMENT AS ART FORM.

HAIDA

THAT EFFORT IS NOW WHOLLY PAST.
EVEN MEMORY OF IT FADES.

HAIDA

HAIDA

ALREADY
THE FOREST
HAS RECLAIMED
THE TINY CLEARINGS
MEN ONCE MAINTAINED
ALONG THE TWISTING WALLS
OF THIS STORMY COAST.

ONLY A HANDFUL OF POLES
NOW STAND,
OR MORE FREQUENTLY LIE,
IN THE DAMP, LUSH FORESTS.

HAIDA

LIKE THE FALLEN TREES
THEY LIE BESIDE,
THEY HAVE BECOME
THE LIFE-BLOOD OF YOUNGER TREES
GROWING FROM THEIR TRUNKS.

HAIDA

IN A SCENE SUBDUED
BY A MAGNIFICENT MOSS COVERING
AND BY SILENCE,
THEY RETURN TO THE FOREST
THAT GAVE THEM BIRTH.

TSIMSHIAN

TSIMSHIAN

KWAKIUTL

TLINGIT

NOTES ON TRIBAL NAMES AND LOCATIONS OF POLES (PARENTHESIS INDICATES PRESENT LOCATION)

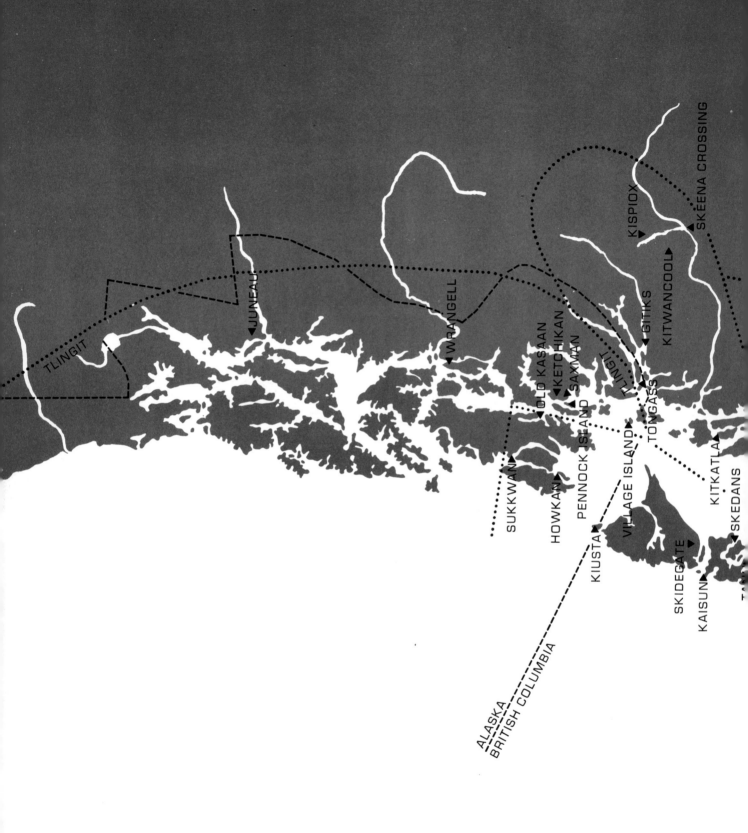

TLINGIT

JUNEAU

WRANGELL

OLD KASAAN
KETCHIKAN
SAXMAN

SUKKWAN

HOWKAN

PENNOCK ISLAND

VILLAGE ISLAND

TLINGIT

TONGASS

GITIKS

KISPIOX

KITWANCOOL

SKEENA CROSSING

KITKATLA

SKIDEGATE

KAISUN

SKEDANS

KIUSTA

ALASKA
BRITISH COLUMBIA

NINSTINTS▶

HAIDA
TSIMSHIAN

BELLA BELLA

TSIMSHIAN
KWAKIUTL

KINGCOME INLET▶

KWAKIUTL

VILLAGE ISLAND▶

TURNOUR ISLAND▶

VANCOUVER▶

··········· TRIBAL BOUNDARIES

‐‐‐‐‐‐‐‐‐‐ NATIONAL BOUNDARIES

ADELAIDE DE MENIL PHOTOGRAPHED IN CAMBODIA, JAPAN, AND THE
BACK COUNTRIES OF BRAZIL AND PERU. SHE WORKED AT THE
AMERICAN MUSEUM OF NATURAL HISTORY, SERVED AS STAFF
PHOTOGRAPHER ON AN ARCHEOLOGICAL EXPEDITION IN GREECE,
AND MOST RECENTLY, SPENT 7 MONTHS FILMING IN NEW GUINEA.

THE PHOTOGRAPHS IN THIS BOOK WERE MADE DURING 1966-68.
SOME OF THE CARVINGS NO LONGER EXIST.

WILLIAM REID'S CARVINGS RIVAL THE FINEST EVER PRODUCED BY
HIS HAIDA FOREBEARS. HIS MOTHER CAME FROM SKIDEGATE, HIS
GRANDMOTHER FROM TANU, THE NOW-VANISHED VILLAGE THAT
WAS ONCE THE CROWNING GEM OF WEST COAST ART.

A NUMBER OF HIS POLES, AND TWO HOUSES, CONSTITUTE THE
CORE OF THE UNIVERSITY OF BRITISH COLUMBIA TOTEM PARK.
DETAILS FROM ONE POLE ARE SHOWN ON PAGES 96-97.

DESIGN BY ARNOLD SKOLNICK

TYPOGRAPHY BY GRAPHO
PRINTING BY RAPOPORT PRINTING CORP.
TYPE FACE: MICROGRAMMA